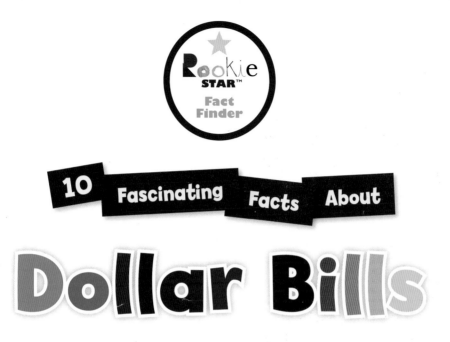

Rookie STAR™
Fact Finder

10 Fascinating Facts About Dollar Bills

by Chris Jozefowicz

Content Consultant
Mark Anderson, Currency Consultant
Museum of American Finance

Reading Consultant
Jeanne M. Clidas, Ph.D.
Reading Specialist

Children's Press®
An Imprint of Scholastic Inc.

Table of Contents

Dollars are the money we use in the United States. Workers are paid with dollars. Shoppers buy things with dollars. And U.S. dollars are one of the most popular **currencies** in the world.

Do you want to learn more fascinating facts about dollar bills? Then read on!

FACT 1

One dollar used to buy a lot more

Today, one dollar is about enough money to buy a chocolate bar. One hundred years ago,

In 1916, a chocolate bar cost just 3 cents.

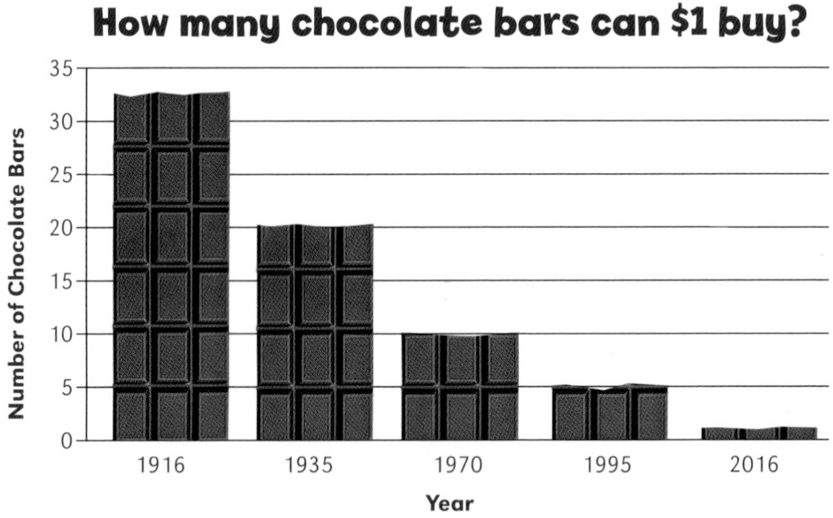

How many chocolate bars can $1 buy?
Number of Chocolate Bars
35
30
25
20
15
10
5
0
1916
1935
1970
1995
2016
Year

that would have bought more than 30 bars! That is because prices almost always go up over time. This process is called **inflation**.

A male deer is called a buck. This may be why we call dollars "bucks," too!

People have used different things as currency over the years. One kind of money was called wampum. It was made from seashells. People also used deerskin as money.

This bill is not made of paper

It may be called paper money, but a dollar is actually made of a mix of cotton and linen. It is stronger than regular paper. A dollar bill can be folded in

Cotton comes from plants.

Most paper would be destroyed in the wash. Not a dollar bill, though!

half forward and backward 4,000 times before it tears! And if your dollar bill goes through the wash, don't worry. It will survive! But you may want to hang it up to dry.

Dollar bills are not printed one at a time. The design is printed onto a big sheet. It fits up to 50 bills. Then the sheets are cut into single bills. More than 10 million bills can be printed each day!

The dollar hides many groups of 13

Look closely at a one-dollar bill. Can you find 13 arrows in an eagle's claw? How about 13 leaves on an olive branch?

There are 13 steps in the pyramid.

13 leaves

13 arrows

Those are just two of many groups of 13. You may be wondering: "Why so many 13s?" They represent the 13 colonies that formed the original United States in 1776.

Some people think there is an owl hidden on the dollar bill. The art is very small. It is on the front top right corner, near the number 1. Other people think it is just part of the background design. What does it look like to you?

This map shows the 13 original American colonies in 1776.

New Hampshire
(Part of Mass.)
New York
Massachusetts
Rhode Island
Connecticut
Pennsylvania
New Jersey
Delaware
Virginia
Maryland
North Carolina
South Carolina
ATLANTIC OCEAN
Georgia

N
W←○→E
S

This bill is really hard to fake

This child is taking a closer look at all the cool features of a dollar bill.

Many things make a dollar bill very hard to **counterfeit**. Try drawing one. It's not easy! There are lots of little red and blue

Look closely. Can you see red and blue threads?

This is prop money used for movies and TV.

You have probably seen people using money in movies. That money is often fake. It usually looks different from real money. That is so it cannot be used in real life. Movie money is usually smaller or larger than real money. And it is printed on only one side.

threads in the paper. The designs have many lines and swirls. The ink is raised. You can feel it with your finger. Explore a dollar with a magnifying glass. Discover its secrets!

There are 11 billion bucks in the world

That is how many one-dollar bills are out in the world at any time. How much money is 11 billion dollars?

You couldn't hold 11 billion dollars in your hand!

Written out, it is $11,000,000,000.00! Each bill weighs about one gram. That is about the same as a single raisin. But 11 billion dollars weighs as much as 850 school buses!

The least common bill is the two-dollar bill. There are about 10 times as many one-dollar bills in the world. Do you have any two-dollar bills? Most people have never received one as change at the store.

The dollar bill honors an American hero

Since the 1860s, portraits of George Washington have appeared on the one-dollar bill. Washington

General George Washington leads his troops.

16

was our first president.
He also led the American
troops in the Revolutionary
War (1775-1783).
After that, he helped
write the Constitution.
Without Washington,
the United States might
not exist.

George's wife, Martha Washington, was added to the one-dollar bill in 1886. She was the first woman on U.S. currency. Her picture was removed when the dollar was redesigned in 1899.

George Washington is known as the "Father of Our Country."

These bills are actually magnetic

Ever wonder how a vending machine knows how much money you put in? The secret is in the ink. Dollar bills have

In real life, a magnet doesn't act like a dollar vacuum!

magnetic ink.
Vending machines can
detect it. Test it yourself.
Hold a dollar gently on one
end. Pass a strong magnet
close to a spot with lots of
ink. The bill should move.

**The ink in
dollar bills**
has small pieces
of iron in it.
Iron is a metal
that responds
to magnets.

Dollars do not last forever

Worn-out bills are shredded.

Most dollar bills last about six years. Sometimes they are too beat up to use. Then the bank sends them to the government for new ones. The government has to print 2.5 million new bills each year to keep up! Some people draw on money. If you find a dollar bill with drawings on it, you can take it to a bank. The bank will give you a new one!

Did you know that all dollars tell you when they were approved for printing? There is a number to the left of Washington's picture. That is the year the bill was approved. Find a dollar. Is it younger than you?

A dollar can be a coin, too

Imagine that all your dollar bills were coins instead. They would probably be harder to carry around!

The first "official" dollar made in the U.S. was a coin. Today, some people want all dollars to be coins again. Right now there are 39 dollar coins with pictures of presidents on them. There is also a golden dollar coin with a picture of Sacagawea. She was an American Indian woman who helped explore western parts of the U.S. in the early 1800s.

The U.S. government has stopped issuing certain large bills. Before 1945, there were bills for $500, $1,000, $5,000, $10,000, even $100,000!

Left to right: President Dwight D. Eisenhower, Susan B. Anthony, Sacagawea

Not all singles are worth one dollar

Some people collect money. Rare dollar bills can be worth much more than a dollar. What makes a bill

Owning a rare bill can make you rich!

A dollar bill's serial number is printed in green.

rare? Some old bills are very rare. Modern bills can also be rare if they have special numbers on them. Each bill has its own serial number. A serial number is like a name. Numbers like 00000000 or 12345678 can be valuable.

One of the most valuable dollar bills is from 1862. That is the first year they were made by the U.S. government. In 2008, this bill sold for $48,875!

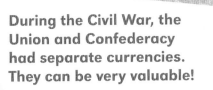

During the Civil War, the Union and Confederacy had separate currencies. They can be very valuable!

Activity
Washington Wings

Follow the instructions below to fold a dollar bill into a glider.

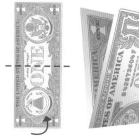

1 Place a dollar bill facedown.

2 Fold the bill in half so the two short ends align at top.

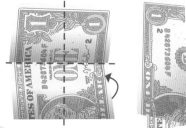

3 Fold the dollar bill in half again so the short ends align at top.

4 Unfold the bill so that it is folded in half again. Fold the bill in half lengthwise, from right to left.

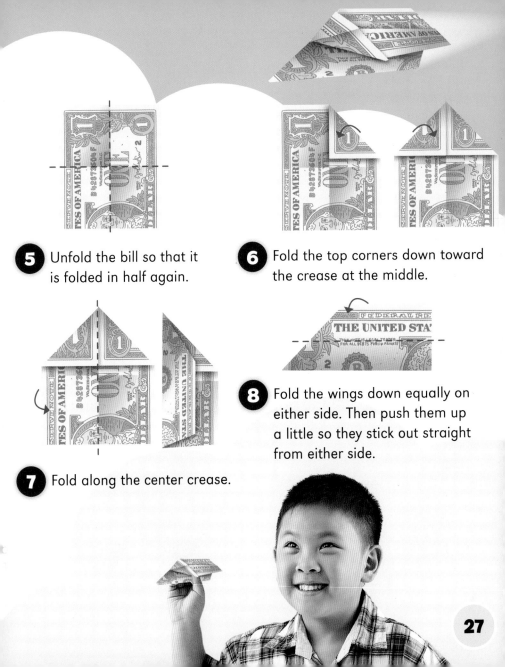

5 Unfold the bill so that it is folded in half again.

6 Fold the top corners down toward the crease at the middle.

7 Fold along the center crease.

8 Fold the wings down equally on either side. Then push them up a little so they stick out straight from either side.

Timeline

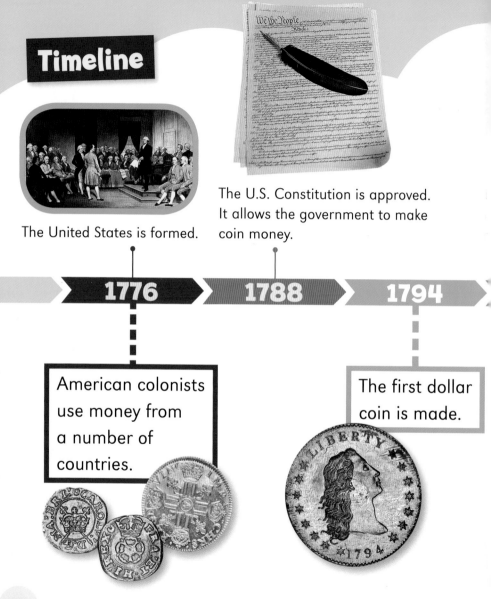

The United States is formed.

The U.S. Constitution is approved. It allows the government to make coin money.

1776

1788

1794

American colonists use money from a number of countries.

The first dollar coin is made.

he Civil War begins. The U.S.
overnment creates bills to have
noney to help pay for the war.

The Civil War ends.

| 1861 | 1862 | 1865 | 1963 |

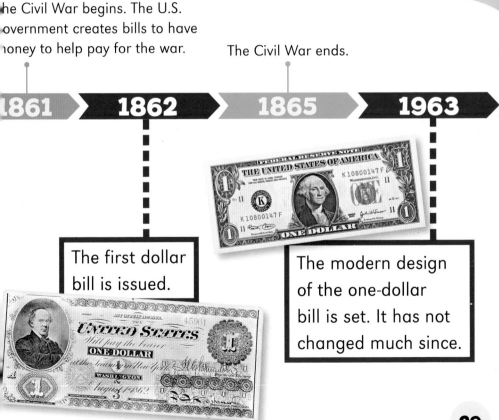

The first dollar bill is issued.

The modern design of the one-dollar bill is set. It has not changed much since.

29

Glossary

- **counterfeit** (KOWNT-uhr-fit): make a fake copy that looks almost like the real thing

- **currencies** (KUR-uhn-seez): forms of money used in a country

- **inflation** (in-FLAY-shun): general increase in prices

- **magnetic** (mag-NET-ik): acting like a magnet, a piece of metal that attracts certain other metals, such as iron

Index

About the Author

Chris Jozefowicz was a scientist who studied things like chicken, frog, and fish brains before he started writing. Since then, he has authored a variety of books and articles for young readers. He lives in Louisville, KY, with his family. He still has a crisp $2 bill from 1976 that his grandmother gave him for his birthday.

Facts for Now

Visit this Scholastic Web site for more information on dollar bills:

www.factsfornow.scholastic.com

Enter the keywords **Dollar Bills**

Library of Congress Cataloging-in-Publication Data

Names: Jozefowicz, Chris, author.
Title: 10 fascinating facts about dollar bills / by Chris Jozefowicz.
Other titles: Ten fascinating facts about dollar bills
Description: New York : Children's Press, an imprint of Scholastic Inc.,
[2016] | Series: Rookie star | Includes bibliographical references and index.
Identifiers: LCCN 2016002789 | ISBN 9780531228159 (library binding : alk. paper) | ISBN 9780531229408 (pbk. : alk. paper)
Subjects: LCSH: Dollar, American—Juvenile literature. | Paper money—United States—Juvenile literature.
Classification: LCC HG591 J69 2016 | DDC 332.4/0440973—dc23 LC record available at http://lccn.loc.gov/2016002789

Produced by Spooky Cheetah Press
Design by Judith Christ-Lafond

© 2017 by Scholastic Inc.

Printed in China 62

SCHOLASTIC, CHILDREN'S PRESS, ROOKIE STAR™ FACT FINDER, and associated logos are trademarks and/or registered trademarks of Scholastic Inc.

1 2 3 4 5 6 7 8 9 10 R 25 24 23 22 21 20 19 18 17 16

Photographs ©: cover girl's face: Roman_Gorielov/Thinkstock; cover girl's body: Lunamarina/Dreamstime; cover dollar bill: aodaodaodaod/Shutterstock, Inc.; cover background: stock09/Shutterstock, Inc.; back cover inset: Dimitri Otis/Getty Images; back cover background: stock09/Shutterstock, Inc.; 2 top right: Michael84/Shutterstock, Inc.; 3 bottom left: paulaphoto/Shutterstock, Inc.; 3 bottom right: Lasse Kristensen/Getty Images; 4-5 background: Suchat Naencharee/Dreamstime; 5 top: malerapaso/Getty Images; 5 bottom: Lyubov Kobyakova/Shutterstock, Inc.; 6: Vasily Kovalev/Shutterstock, Inc.; 7 bottom: Alex Helin/Shutterstock, Inc.; 7 bottom grass: Fedorov Oleksiy/Shutterstock, Inc.; 7 top purse: Robyn Mackenzie/Shutterstock, Inc.; 7 top shells: Lizard/Shutterstock, Inc.; 8: Australian Scenics/Getty Images; 9 top left: Steven Puetzer/Getty Images; 9 top right: Bloomberg/Getty Images; 10 dollar bill and throughout: Didier Kobi/Dreamstime; 11 top right owl: Rosa Jay/Shutterstock, Inc.; 12 left: 3445128471/Shutterstock, Inc.; 12 center dollar bill: Dave Bredeson/ Dreamstime; 12 right: Paul J. Richards/Getty Images; 13: LHB Photo/Alamy Images; 14 left: iCreative3D/Shutterstock, Inc.; 14 bottom right boy: sashahaltam/Shutterstock, Inc.; 14 bottom right dollar bill: Dave Bredeson/Dreamstime; 14 bottom right raisin: EM Arts/Shutterstock, Inc.; 15 top right: Lipskiy/Shutterstock, Inc.; 15 bottom: sashahaltam/Shutterstock, Inc.; 16: Don Troiani/Corbis Images; 17 bottom portrait: Superstock, Inc.; 17 bottom frame: gillmar/Shutterstock, Inc.; 17 top right: Universal History Archive/Getty Images; 18 bottom left: Asier Romero/Shutterstock, Inc.; 18-19 dollar bills: Pedro Moniz/Shutterstock, Inc.; 19 top right: MilanB/Shutterstock, Inc.; 20 center left: rsooll/Shutterstock, Inc.; 20-21 bottom: Africa Studio/Fotolia; 21 center left: Sofi photo/Shutterstock, Inc.; 22: Valery Sidelnykov/Shutterstock, Inc.; 23 top left: Heritage Auctions/Splash/Newscom; 23 top center: Scott Olson/ Getty Images; 23 top right: Helen H. Richardson/Getty Images; 23 bottom left: Asaf Eliason/Shutterstock, Inc.; 23 bottom center: maogg/iStockphoto; 23 bottom right: Scott Rothstein/ Shutterstock, Inc.; 24 bottom left: wavebreakmedia/Shutterstock, Inc.; 25 top right: Corbis Images; 25 bottom right: The Granger Collection; 25 bottom left: The Granger Collection; 26 illustrations: Keith Plechaty; 27 bottom right: DragonImages/Fotolia; 27 illustrations: Keith Plechaty; 28 top left: SuperStock/Getty Images; 28 bottom right: Hurst Photo/Shutterstock, Inc.; 28 bottom left: zzubra/Fotolia; 28 bottom center: De Agostini/G. Dagli Orti/Getty Images; 28 bottom right: PRNewsFoto/Stack's Bowers Galleries/AP Images; 29 top: Augustus A. Tholey/Library of Congress; 29 bottom left: Corbis Images; 30 top: Freer Law/Thinkstock; 30 center bottom: Hurst Photo/Shutterstock, Inc.; 30 center top: wavebreakmedia/ Shutterstock, Inc.; 30 bottom: MilanB/Shutterstock, Inc.

Maps by Jim McMahon.